# Haunted Britain
## Daniel Blythe

## Contents

Badger
LEARNING

## Vocabulary

exposure

mysteriously

paranormal

sceptics

scrawled

séances

suffocated

techniques

# 1. Britain's most haunted

Britain is full of ghost stories and legends.

People claim to have seen spooky figures in old castles, in ruined manor houses and even just on ordinary staircases.

Sometimes they say they also hear terrible screeching, or they claim to have caught a ghost on camera.

### Harmless hauntings

People say they have felt a touch on their shoulder or an icy chill down their spine.

But most ghost-hunters agree that, while ghosts are frightening, they never do any actual harm to anyone.

**WOW!** facts

Pengersick Castle in Cornwall is one of England's most haunted places. They say it has over 20 ghosts including a monk, a woman who walks through walls, and a boy who tugs on people's clothes.

The village of Pluckley, in Kent, is famous as the most haunted village in England.

Its ghosts include:

- The Red Lady, looking for the grave of her dead baby.

- The Watercress Lady, who burned to death when her pipe set her whisky on fire!

- The Colonel of Park Woods, who hanged himself in woodland near Pluckley. People see him there at dusk, in his full soldier's uniform.

- The Highwayman, who used to lie in wait for travellers in a hollow tree at a place known as Fright Corner.

Whether the stories are true or not – and many think they are just a bit of spooky fun – they are certainly good for tourism…

# Highwayman of Fright Corner Dead
## DuBois' Reign Of Terror Ends

Horrid highwayman Robert DuBois, who brought terror to the people of Pluckley, is finally no more.

The robber was found dead in the early hours of Monday morning, pinned by a spear to the oak tree at Fright Corner – the same tree where he would lie in wait for his victims.

It is thought that DuBois' killer could have been a Guard of the Law, or maybe even a rival thief who knew of his hiding place.

# 2. Restless souls and friendly ghosts

Ghosts are often linked with people who died in nasty or violent ways.

Some people think spirits are 'restless' because of how they died, or that they have come back to seek revenge on their killers!

They say the Tower of London is haunted by dozens of souls who met their grisly fate there.

These include the young Princes in the Tower, who probably died there in 1483, and Henry VIII's fifth wife, Catherine Howard, who was executed in 1542.

In the 17th century, a deadly plague called the Black Death spread through the country.

In 1665, the people of Eyam in Derbyshire cut themselves off completely so that other villages nearby were not infected.

Today, people hear strange footsteps in the local pub, the Miners Arms. People also claim to have seen the ghost of Sarah Mills, a servant girl who died in the village well.

Borley Rectory in Essex is often called the most haunted house in England.

Since 1929, people have reported all kinds of different spooks in the house – ghostly footsteps, strange lights, a headless man and the figure of a nun, among many other strange things.

In the 1930s, Marianne Foyster lived in Borley with her husband who was the vicar.

She claimed she was slapped by invisible hands, and nearly suffocated by a mattress. She also said she saw scrawled messages on the walls that just appeared.

Invisible ghosts which crash about and throw objects are called poltergeists. This word comes from German, meaning 'noisy spirit'.

One of the most haunted places in Scotland is Edinburgh Castle.

People say they have seen:
- a phantom bagpipe player
- a drummer
- dozens of former prisoners

In 2001 a team of 'ghostbusters', led by Dr Richard Wiseman from the University of Hertfordshire, explored the castle.

Did they find any ghosts?

- They saw shadowy figures.
- They thought they were being watched.
- They felt extremes of heat and cold.

But nobody saw an actual ghost.

### Culloden Moor

Culloden Moor, near Inverness, is where the last battle on British soil was fought on 16th April, 1746.

Over 2000 men lost their lives in the battle and many who were injured died from their wounds.

Every 16th April, the moaning, bloodied ghosts of soldiers rise from the ground, they say.

People hear cries of battle and the clash of swords.

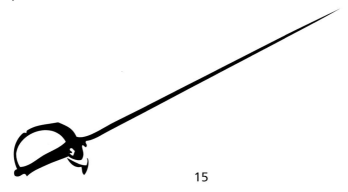

Another place with a grim history is the Skirrid Inn, the oldest pub in Wales.

It was used as a courtroom in the 1800s, and over 180 criminals were hanged there. The pub holds 'ghost hunts' when people stay overnight to catch a chance of seeing a ghost.

Some people say they see the ghosts of the judge and the hangman. Some people report feeling ill, and some even say they can feel a noose tightening round their necks!

Ghosts don't always cause fear and panic.

In another famous haunted house in Wales, Miskin Manor, a ghostly lady appears in the bar between midnight and 1am.

The owners are quite used to her – and the night porter just nods hello to her!

# 3. Creepy castles, headless horrors

Britain is full of ruined castles and crumbling abbeys, which are ideal settings for the ghosts of old soldiers, lords, ladies, kings and queens to be spotted.

Anne Boleyn was the second wife of King Henry VIII for just three years. When he grew tired of her, he had her head chopped off.

Hever Castle in Kent was where Anne grew up. Every Christmas her ghost is supposed to appear walking across the bridge where she and Henry went courting.

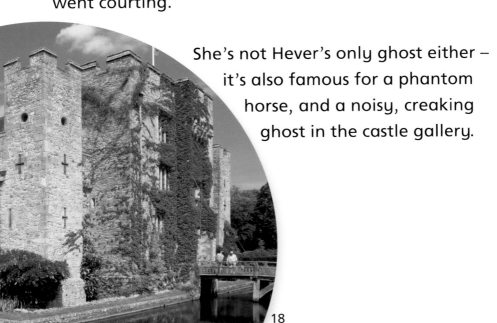

She's not Hever's only ghost either – it's also famous for a phantom horse, and a noisy, creaking ghost in the castle gallery.

18

Belgrave Hall in Leicestershire is said to be home to many ghosts.

One is the ghost of a Victorian lady who people say wears a bright, blood-red dress.

Other visitors to Belgrave Hall say they have heard footsteps but there is no one there and doors slam closed when no one has touched them.

Some people find the rides at Alton Towers theme park really scary but they are not as scary as nearby Alton Towers house.

The house is popular with ghost hunters because of the number of sightings of ghosts and strange happenings:

- People say they have heard the sound of footsteps along an empty corridor.

- Other people reported they heard stones being thrown but there was nobody there to throw them.

- Lots of people say they have seen a lady in a long dress walking along the corridors. She looks so lifelike that some people thought she was a real visitor.

In Victorian times, posh ladies used to have séances where they said they could make contact with the dead. They sat around a Ouija board printed with the alphabet. A glass mysteriously moved to spell out words.

Often, ghosts seem to turn up in remote, misty places with their own special atmosphere.

In Laugharne in South Wales there is a boathouse which was owned by Welsh poet, Dylan Thomas.

The boathouse is now haunted by the poet's mother, Florence. It's said you can hear her scraping a chair across the floor upstairs at night – while visitors to the boathouse often find lights switched off, and books and pictures moved.

Another spooky place is the harbour town of Whitby in Yorkshire.

In the story of Dracula, he sailed to Whitby.

In the ruined abbey, which stands high above the town, people claim to have seen the image of the abbey's founder, the Abbess Hild. They say she appears wrapped in the clothes she was buried in.

Other hauntings in Whitby include the Barguest Coach, pulled by phantom horses. It is full of skeleton sailors.

Not all ghosts are knights, monks, or lords and ladies from past centuries.

Some of Britain's most famous hauntings involve people who died in the last few decades. There are groups on Facebook with a special interest in modern-day ghost sightings.

These ghosts don't wear long cloaks or ride around in coaches. They wear jeans and hoodies!

## The Devil's bonfires

If you walk through the Haunted Valley of Longdendale in the Derbyshire Peak District at dusk, you may hear strange howling sounds and see spooky lights called the 'Devil's bonfires'.

**WOW! facts**

In the ancient Ram Inn, Gloucestershire, some guests said they heard the screams of a girl called Rosie who had been murdered long ago. The guests were so scared they jumped out of the window!

# 4. Believers versus sceptics

### All in the mind?

So, are ghosts real? It's fair to say most people treat ghost stories as just a bit of fun.

There are lots of people who don't believe in ghosts. They say there is no proof. Such people are called sceptics. They think that people who say they have seen a ghost are only imagining it.

### Fearless fakers

Much of the 'evidence' for ghosts has been shown to be fake. With old cameras, people could always fake photos using a double exposure, where two photos are mixed together.

Today, it's even easier using digital cameras and technology. You could do it yourself very easily, on a computer at home or school! Sounds can be faked with modern techniques too.

One photo seems to show a ghostly girl in a fire in Wem. However, the photo was a trick, as the same girl appears in a postcard of Wem High Street from the 1920s.

## Ghost hunters

There are people who make it their hobby to seek out spooky experiences!

Groups of ghost hunters meet up to spend the night in haunted houses, and discuss sightings on the internet.

Some groups offer special events and 'fright nights' where people can sign up to be involved – although they can't promise that you will see or hear anything spooky!

Sometimes, though, they get lucky.

**WOW!** facts

Magician James Randi has offered $1 million to anyone who can prove that their paranormal sighting is real. So far, Randi's $1 million has stayed in the bank!

Societies like SpookSavers even put eerie voices and photos up on their websites for everyone to enjoy.

People can decide for themselves if they are sights and sounds of actual ghosts!

# 5. Britain's top 10 haunted places

| Number | Place | Ghosts | Fear Factor |
|---|---|---|---|
| 10. | Berry Pomeroy Castle, Devon | White Lady, Blue Lady | ☠ |
| 9. | Tower of London | Executed prisoners, Catherine Howard, Princes in the Tower | ☠☠ |
| 8. | Culloden Moor, Scotland | Dead Jacobite soldiers | ☠☠ |
| 7. | The Skirrid Inn, Wales | Hanged criminals, the Hangman and the Judge | ☠☠☠ |
| 6. | Edinburgh Castle, Scotland | Phantom piper, drummer, prisoners | ☠☠☠ |
| 5. | Glamis Castle, Scotland | Many including the Monster of Glamis | ☠☠☠ |
| 4. | The Ancient Ram Inn, Gloucestershire | Little Rosie | ☠☠☠☠ |
| 3. | Pendle Hill, Lancashire | Hanged witches | ☠☠☠☠ |
| 2. | Borley Rectory, Essex | Poltergeists, nun, headless man | ☠☠☠☠ |
| 1. | Pluckley, Kent | Many including the Red Lady, the Colonel and the Highwayman | ☠☠ |

## Questions

Where is Britain's most haunted village? *(page 7)*

Who are the ghosts of Culloden, and how did they die? *(page 15)*

Which famous person is said to haunt Hever Castle? *(page 18)*

What ghost can be found at Alton Towers? *(page 21)*

How was the ghost of the girl in the fire shown to be a fake? *(page 27)*

Do you think ghosts are real? Can we ever prove it one way or the other?

# Index